To Leo Alexander
who inspired me to make this book
and who inspires me every day.

A family, at home,
in their apartment.

A child woke up
one day and asked
to sing the alphabet.

A child woke
up one day and
asked to learn
about some
animals.

This child was told that
his wish would come
true and Mommy, Daddy
and child went on
an adventure.

A is for

Armadillo

An Armadillo's whole body is covered with bony plates, natural armor!

B is for

Baboon

Baboons use 30 varied sounds for communication. They can grunt, scream and even bark. They also yawn, smack their lips or shrug their shoulders to communicate.

D is for

Dolphin

Dolphins are playful. They jump out of the water and ride waves for fun.

G is for

Gecko

Geckos have tiny hooks on their feet acting like suction cups. Some can crawl on surfaces such as ceilings and walls without falling off.

H is for

Hippopotamus

Hippopotamuses are often found resting in water because water helps keep their temperature down.

I is for

Indri Lemur

Indri lemurs are herbivores, which mean they only eat plant based food.

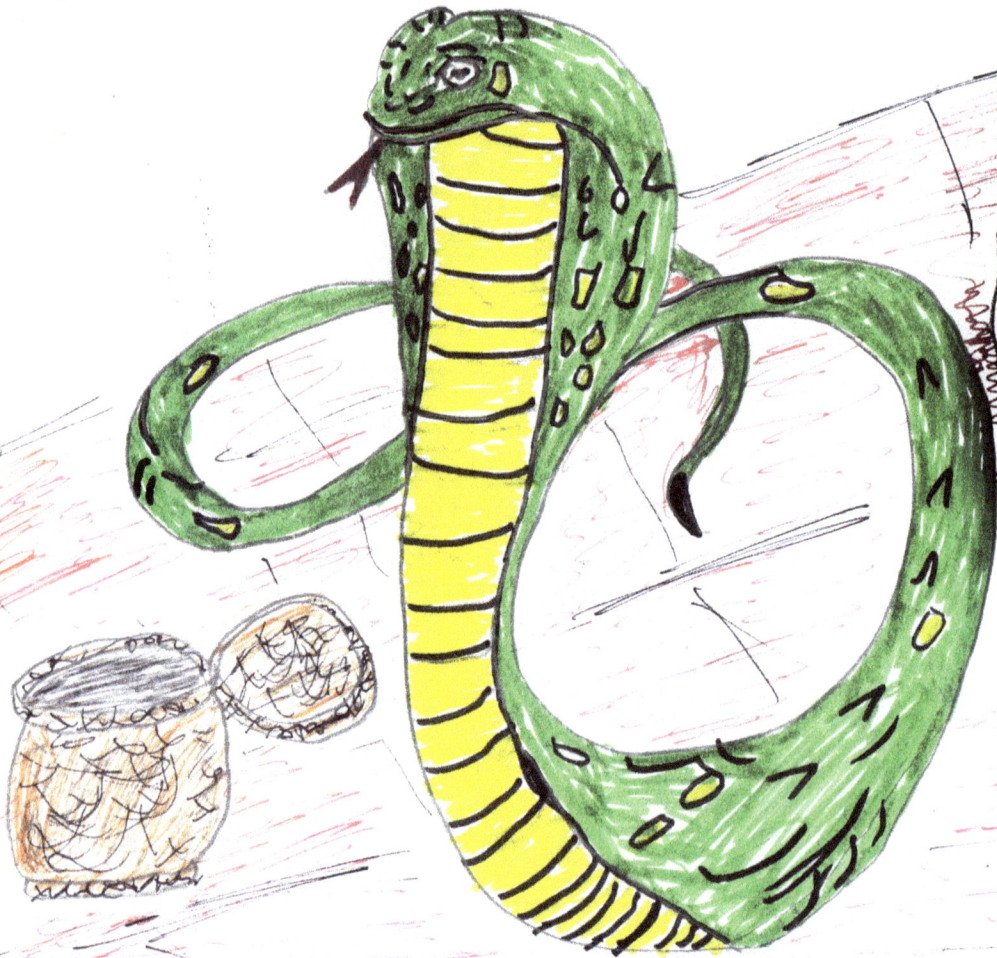

N is for

Nightingale
Nightingales are named due to their habit of singing during the night and early morning.

P is for

Penguin

Penguins safely drink sea water. Their bodies remove the salt in the water.

Q is for

Quokka

Quokkas are nocturnal, which means they are active at night when it's cooler.

R is for

Raccoon

Raccoons are solitary, which means they live on their own.

U is for urial

An urial's wool is reddish brown that fades in the winter.

W is for Wasp

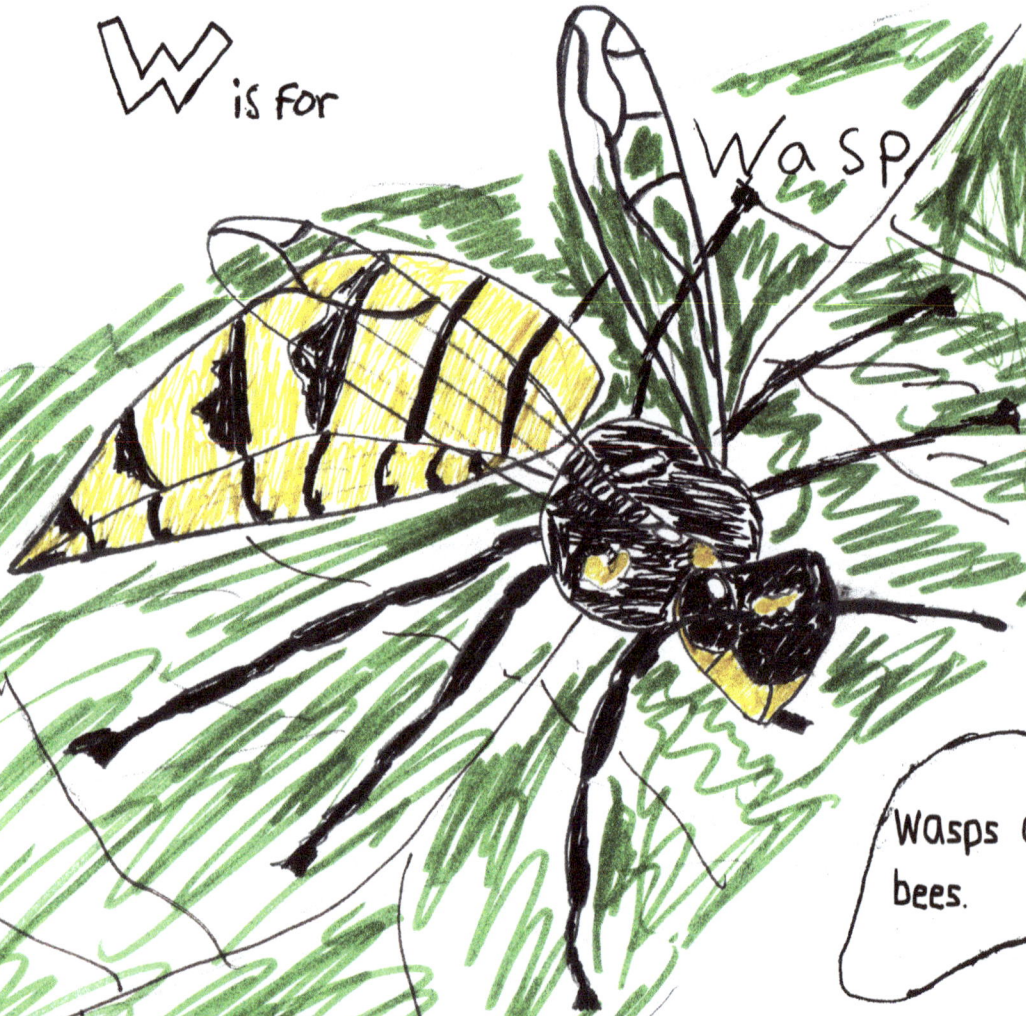

Wasps are n
bees.

Z is for

Zebra

Every zebra has its own pattern of black and white stripes.

Child
Oh my, how my wish came true.
Oh how I'd like to thank you two!
Parents
We'd do anything for you.
Oh how much we do love you.

www.ingramcontent.com/pod-product-compliance
Lightning Source LLC
Chambersburg PA
CBHW040252100426
42811CB00011B/1234